MASTHEAD

MW01167410

Steve Daniels
EXECUTIVE DIRECTOR

Myles Estey
EDITOR-IN-CHIEF

Santos Henarejos
ART DIRECTOR

Gema Navarro
ART DIRECTOR

Melanie Chow
BUSINESS DIRECTOR

Justin Levinson
INSTITUTE DIRECTOR

Maria Gallucci
FEATURES EDITOR

Alexia Liakounakou
ASSOCIATE EDITOR

Eli Rosenbloom
DESIGN CONSULTANT

Stephanie Davidson
ILLUSTRATION EDITOR

Matt Peters
VIDEO EDITOR

Matt Prindible
RESEARCH ASSOCIATE

**Miguel de
la Fuente-Lau**
COMMUNITY MANAGER

David Steinberg
COMMUNITY MANAGER

April Zhu
COMMUNITY MANAGER

Editorial Board

Zach Hyman
MYANMAR

Amanda Mustard
EGYPT

Philippa Young
LEBANON

Website
mkshft.org

Twitter, Facebook,
Instagram, YouTube
@mkshftmag
#hiddencreativity

Makeshift is published
independently by Makeshift
Media, dedicated to uncovering
creative solutions from the
economic fringe.
mkshft.org/about

Art direction provided by Rifle,
a graphic design studio with no
fixed base, focused on editorial
projects around the world.
wearerifle.com

Printing by the Prolific Group,
an eco-friendly printer in
Winnipeg, Canada. Makeshift
is printed on FSC-certified
Cougar Opaque 80-lb. cover and
Lynx Opaque 70-lb. text.
prolific.ca

Distribution by Ubiquity,
Central Books, MMS, and New
Distribution House and stocked
in hundreds of stores globally.
Visit your local store and tell
them about us. If you're looking
to stock Makeshift or purchase
a bulk order, visit our site or
contact one of our distributors.
mkshft.org/stockists

In partnership with:

openbox

GE

If you would like to partner with
Makeshift visit
mkshft.org/partner

Cover photo by Jan Chipchase

Contributors

Jan Chipchase
KABUL, AFGHANISTAN
Jan is the founder of the discreet global research, strategy, and design consultancy, Studio D Radiodurans.
@janchip
— Cover

Adam Cohn
WONOCOLO, INDONESIA
Adam is a freelance photographer and avid traveler based in Seattle.
adamcohn.com
— Black Gold Market, p. 22

Chris Duffy
BOSTON, US
Chris is a writer and the producer/host of the new public radio program You're the Expert.
@chrisiduffy
— Brain Waves, p. 62

Myles Estey
MEXICO CITY, MEXICO
Myles is Editor-in-Chief of Makeshift and a freelance journalist and producer covering Mexico and Central America.
@esteyonage
— Editor's Note, p. 04

Duncan Forgan
BANGKOK, THAILAND
Duncan is a freelance editor, writer, and broadcaster covering Thailand, Vietnam, and the rest of Southeast Asia.
duncankarol.com
— Pocket Protectors, p. 32

James Fredrick
MEXICO CITY, MEXICO
James is a street food enthusiast and business reporter in Mexico City focused on energy.
@jameslfredrick
— Streetside Shocks, p. 90

Maria Gallucci
BROOKLYN, US
Maria is the Features Editor of Makeshift and an energy and environment reporter based in New York City.
@mariagallucci
— DIY Fusion, p. 28
— Tesla's Tower, p. 76

Zach Hyman
SHANGHAI, CHINA
Zach pursues interesting design research opportunities, from talking with farmers in Myanmar to chasing tractors across China. He now studies design at Carnegie Mellon.
squareinchanthro.com
— Hybrid Haulers, p. 58

Payal Khandelwal
RAJASTHAN, INDIA
Payal is a freelance visual communications journalist and writer based out of India.
@thefloatingbed
— One-Liter Farming, p. 18

Justin Levinson
NEW YORK, US
Justin is Director of the Makeshift Institute, teaching students and companies to uncover hidden creativity. He is a maker at heart, a career generalist with engineering tendencies.
@justin_levinson
— Joule Thieves, p. 72

Humberto Márquez
CARACAS, VENEZUELA
Humberto is a Venezuelan journalist focusing on international affairs. He is a correspondent for Inter Press Service, contributor for Radio Netherlands, and columnist for El Nacional.
@hmarquez26
— Combustible Contraband, p. 52

Amanda Mustard
CAIRO, EGYPT
Amanda is a self-taught photojournalist raised on a Christmas tree farm in Pennsylvania and based in Cairo, with a fondness for film scores, pomegranates, and tattoos.
amandamustardphoto.com
— Observed, p. 66

Rose Odengo
NAIROBI, KENYA
Rose is a young African woman tired of being a victim. She's on a rampage for change one story at a time.
@anneodengo
— Poo Power, p. 84

Alex Potter
SANA'A, YEMEN
Alex is a photojournalist based in Yemen, always on the move for stories from the Middle East to the Midwest.
@alexkpotter
— Leafy Buzz, p. 86

Tara Rice
TIMBUKTU, MALI
Tara is a freelance photographer based in Brooklyn, NY.
tararicephoto.com
— Solar Boom, p. 94

Raphael Wright
DETROIT, US
Raphael is a Detroit-based entrepreneur, author of the street hustling handbook How 2 Hustle, and designer of HustleMania Shirts.
@rafa_ox313
— Grid Grab, p. 68

Contents

Professional cyclists, amongst the most efficient of human power plants, generate an average of around 250 watts during a grueling Tour de France stage. In dead sprints, they can generate up to an impressive 2,000 watts—enough to power up about a dozen laptops or two average US households over their short strides.

With the amount of energy-consuming devices that make up the modern world, this is merely a spark, to say the least. We have become energy obsessed and constructed the world to meet the needs of gadgets and gizmos, from basic lighting to complex machines. An average Chinese coal-fired power plant (of which there are roughly 600) can put out 600 million watts, while the Hoover Dam in the western US has a max output of 2 billion watts. The global population needs the equivalent of some 350 Hoover Dams to maintain everyone's metabolism at a functional, resting state.

Tracking numbers across the energy spectrum is a staggering task and helps us understand the problem. But Makeshift keeps its eyes on the ground level, where small-scale innovators reimagine the ways of making, moving, and using energy—the three processes that form the chapters of this issue. From waste treatment used to produce methane cooking gas in urban Nairobi to artisanal oil mining in rural Indonesia, from a DIY reactor anywhere you want to build it to grid grabbers in Detroit—we came across ingenious solutions.

The energy we need each day goes beyond kilowatts. While countless millions require the jolt of caffeine to face the daily grind, drugs of all kinds promise energy-alteration, and (especially for those of the illegal sort) great effort to deliver them. In the dark of night, pictured right, smugglers lash alcohol to the back of horses, risking the journey across the border to

Iran, where it is prohibited. Another addictive substance, oil, makes the return journey.

On other pages, Honduran prisoners process cocaine, and a Beninese mixologist adds vipers to the moonshine he hawks. Fairfield, Iowa, turns out to be the improbable epicenter of Transcendental Meditation, where practitioners believe their daily routines help charge their own batteries and transmit positivity to society at large.

Still other innovations hold the potential to address some of the world's greatest challenges: food security—finding enough calories to feed multiplying mouths—and climate change—a phenomenon that demands we both ditch fossil fuels for cleaner energy sources and adapt to a changing planet.

This issue marks three full years of Makeshift staff and contributors using their energy to scour the globe for stories of surprising ingenuity. Needless to say, we are thrilled to be thriving as an independent publisher, and we know we have a lot more to bring. If our work over this time has taught us anything, it's that some of the best and brightest ideas for the future will come from people and places we least expect—some just need that extra jolt to amplify their work to the next level.

Myles Estey
EDITOR-IN-CHIEF

Smugglers attach boxes of alcohol to their horses before taking their goods across the border into Iran. Iranian Kurds smuggle cheap petrol from Iran into Iraq in exchange for alcohol in the opposite direction. In 2009, the Iranian military shot and killed at least four smugglers and 600 horses in an attempt to keep alcohol out of the Islamic republic.
Photo: Sebastian Meyer

These are stories of creativity that inspire our team. Find more ideas fresh From the Makery on our Facebook and Twitter streams or in your inboxes weekly.

mkshft.org   @mkshftmag   #fromthemakery

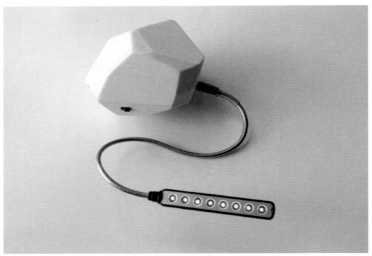

Marina Shacola

Organic banking
ETHIOPIA

Three decades ago, Ethiopia shocked the world with a famine that killed more than a million people. Since then, scientists and farmers have made progress in tackling food insecurity. Hundreds of agricultural training centers, with the backing of both governmental and non-governmental organizations, have succeeded in keeping farmers informed amid temperature swings. Yet in a serious dry spell, no amount of knowledge can sprout new seeds. To combat this risk, Ethiopians have created 18 seed banks across the populous and drought-prone Oromia and Amhara zones. With the source of human calories on the line, preparation seems the best approach.

Shake it like a...
KENYA

Because three-quarters of Kenyans lack access to sustainable electricity, percussionist Sudha Kheterpal, from the group Faithless, raised more than USD 90,000 on Kickstarter to create a musical instrument that doubles as a source of clean energy. The fist-sized polygonal box, manufactured to imitate sounds of traditional African instruments, works by shaking—convenient for music making. The box has two compartments: one holds the beads that reverberate to make sound, and the other contains two magnets placed on each end of a coil and an attached battery. When shaken, the magnets create a current that passes through the coil and charges the battery. Through the external USB plug on the box, users—regardless of connection to dependable electrical grids—can charge their light, phone, or music player or simply take it along. The creators say they don't know what the device will cost yet, but if priced right, it could shake up the energy market.

shakeyourpower.com

③

Death-proof

NIGERIA

Resisting Boko Haram's attackers is no easy task. The group, said to be better armed and trained than much of Nigeria's army, poses a growing threat to residents of the country's northeast. Since machetes, stones, and sticks proved unsuccessful in keeping the hardline militia away, local residents began to look elsewhere. Vigilante groups enhanced their defense by assembling their own weaponry from spare car parts, cobbled together with scrap wood. Noting the shortcomings in this approach, residents sought further reinforcements: bulletproofing. Though not your average military-issue kevlar vest, wearers believe the approach to be effective. Following centuries-old traditions, protective amulets have been revived in hopes of letting the spirits tackle the violence. In Maiduguri, elder practitioners stitch leather amulets that tuck under the shirts of those on the front lines, hoping the amulets can stop Boko Haram one bullet at a time.

Alice Pattullo

④

CARBON-FREE CARS

NIGERIA

OAU Peeps

Worried about all the carbon dioxide spewing from his petroleum-burning engine, Segun Oyeyiola sought a cleaner way to get around town. So he retrofitted a Volkswagen Beetle to run on sunrays and wind gusts instead. The top of the bug's green metal frame carries a giant rectangular solar panel, which charges a battery in the back of the car. A wind turbine sits under the hood, so that when air flows through the grille and the rotors turn, it similarly boosts the battery. As an engineering student at Obafemi Awolowo University in southwestern Nigeria, Segun says he built the carbon-free car partly with free scrap parts donated by friends. The rest cost him less than USD 6,000—inspiration, he says, to make this the future of driving in diesel-fume-heavy Nigeria.

bit.ly/1t9MEPI

⑤

Self-generating gym

UK

Counting calories while burning up the elliptical? With up to dozens of spandexed clients pushing their limits on their machines at any given time, some gym owners have caught on to the basic math that a surplus of potential power lies at their fingertips. This is not new: many gyms have owned machines powered by exercise for years. Cadbury Gym, however, takes it to a new level. With a storage unit called a dynamo, energy flows from the thighs back into the building's electrical grid, dropping the carbon footprint and the utility bill—while offering an extra incentive for clients to push just a little harder.

Jailpreneurship

BOLIVIA

La Paz's San Pedro is unlike most prisons. As an inmate, you can order a prostitute, open your own restaurant, bring your family over to stay with you, or even rent a luxury cell—it all depends on whether or not you have the cash. Even quarrels are solved by representatives elected by the inmates themselves. Perfect prison democracy or total anarchy (depending on one's point of view), prisoners are free to do as they please, provided that they don't leave San Pedro. Numerous labs produce San Pedro's famous homebrewed cocaine in large quantities and, according to visitors, top-notch quality. For more details, the story of Liverpool-born Thomas McFadden—who spent four-and-a-half years in San Pedro, turning his jail-time into a thriving business of manufacturing the addictive powder and shipping it into the illegal economy—will soon come to the big screen.

Danielle Pereira

Nuclear undo

JAPAN

The Renewable Energy Village, a community initiative in Fukushima, is currently under construction in farmland previously contaminated by radiation from the nearby nuclear plant in 2011. The project aims to promote autonomous, solar-powered electricity and revive farming beneath the raised photovoltaic panels. The plant of choice is the rapeseed, which, according to Belarusian scientists, absorbs radionuclides while leaving the food uncontaminated. With 120 panels generating 30 kilowatts already in action and plans to install wind turbines on deck, it's all systems go. The main question remaining is how the farmers might be affected by radioactive elements still lurking in the soil.

Coco fuel

PAPUA NEW GUINEA

When mining giant Rio Tinto blockaded the Papua New Guinean island of Bougainville in 1990 for forcibly closing its mine, outside goods became nearly impossible to acquire. For life to go on, innovation had to happen. Turning to local foods was easy enough—manufactured goods and fuel, less so. Not to be discouraged, residents quickly identified coconuts—plentiful in the island nation—as a reasonable composite for fuel. And, with enough tinkering, the coconut's oil quickly kept the trucks running until the blockade lifted.

FOWL FUEL

USA

What do you do with 11 billion pounds of annual poultry waste—besides stuffing duvets? Right now, the massive amount of feathers, blood, and innards goes mostly into cheap animal food. But scientists at the University of Nevada thought up a new and environmentally friendly formula to create biodiesel out of our winged friends' pulverized-down and spare entrails. The process involves extracting fat from the chicken's remains using boiling water and processing it into biodiesel. Today, the world produces around 33.6 billion gallons of biodiesel annually, extracted from natural vegetable oils and animal fat. Given the abundance of poultry, biodiesel generated from chicken fat could contribute up to 2 percent, or 593 million gallons, to the 33.6 billion gallon total. The researchers also note that the removal of fat from chickens before canning them into pet foods results in both higher-quality animal feed and a better nitrogen source for fertilizer applications. Power in feathers, coming soon to an engine near you.

Rona Binay

Sam Scholes

Winds of autonomy

USA

Facing chronic poverty and underemployment, an estimated 40 percent of the South Dakota's Oglala Lakota tribe lack access to electricity. This is not an isolated problem. With Native American homes often scattered miles off the utility grid, their owners have come to a realization: cooperate and improvise or be left in the dark. Some communities are embracing local, renewable energy as a means to do just this, while creating jobs and tackling income problems their communities face. Arizona's Hopi tribe spearheaded the energy run back in 1987 by forming the Hopi Solar Electric Enterprise, which sold and fitted small-scale solar systems for households in the region. The Navajo created the Navajo Tribal Utility Authority (NTUA) in 1999, which rents access to photovoltaic systems and solar-wind hybrid systems. The Moapa Band of Paiutes recently completed a 250-megawatt hybrid microgrid project, and Tuntutuliak, a town in Western Alaska home to 400 Yup'ik residents, installed a 450-kilowatt wind-diesel hybrid project to power the town and lower the costs of energy consumption.

POOP ZAPPER

USA

Researchers at the University of Colorado say they are "reinventing the toilet" to make sanitation cleaner and safer around the world. The group's solar-thermal toilet transforms human excrement into sterilized bio-charcoal. Dubbed "Sol-Char," the latrine-like contraption contains a reaction chamber, which beams in tropical sunbeams through fiber-optic cables and zaps the human waste inside to 315 degrees Celsius. Once heated, the poop transforms into small black briquettes that burn just like regular charcoal and are used to fertilize cropland. Sol-Char's makers—backed by the Bill & Melinda Gates Foundation—say the project could serve the 40 percent of people worldwide who don't have a sustainable waste treatment system.
— Bayla Metzger

facebook.com/
solarbiochar

Jock Gill

Andres Lozano Martin

Power nap

GLOBAL

Got that 2 p.m. feeling? Science says it's natural; most mammals nap, and so should we. One NASA study concluded that even pilots should take a nap in-flight—alongside an alert co-pilot, of course. Those with a bit of shut-eye improved performance by 34 percent, the scientists found. How about the rest of us? If you're an early riser, consider a nap around 1:30 or 2; otherwise, 2:30 or 3. The duration? A Cornell study says a 20-minute nap will give you a zap of alertness, while one at Harvard claims a 45-minute doze will improve cognitive memory processing. In most cases, you should stop it right there, though, or else you'll fall into 'slow-wave,' or 'deep,' sleep and wake up groggy. If you do need more time, stretch it out to 90–120 minutes for the full cycle of deep and REM sleep. The power nap is back in full force.

Geo cookout
ICELAND

Often championed for its ability to be energy independent, Iceland's vast reserves of geothermal activity are also available for your own private cookout. While bathers douse themselves in the more tepid pools, chefs keep an eye out for the hotter patches of steam. Here, eggs can boil as they float between rocks. Cook trays can rest atop rocks, where anything from cinnamon buns to potato latkes can fry to perfection. And—if you can find a stick in the barren landscape—skewered hot dogs can heat above the rising, boiling steam: a campfire without the coals.

Foggy digs

INDIA

Coal meets two-thirds of India's energy needs. With consumption this high, many people professionally (yet illegally) double as coal diggers to make a living. In Jharia, Jharkhand, coal is so abundant that thousands of residents dig it out from open-pit mines to sell in local markets. Paying about USD 4 a day, it brings a lot more to the table than farming. Miners rarely follow regulations, which require filling a depleted mine with earth over debris and rocks, then planting trees atop to replenish the land. But illegal profits come with costs. Blasting has created cracks in both the soil and houses in the region, underground fires risk igniting below inhabited areas, and gas and dust emissions pollute the air and water. A simultaneously lucrative and hazardous side-job, its importance to local energy needs is undeniable.

Hakbong Kwon

DESERT SCULPTURES
UK
AND EGYPT

Sun, sand, and a 3D printer. Markus Kayser, a student at the Royal College of Art, experimented with these in the Sahara to prove that his new 3D technology dubbed solar sintering may be all you need if you're stuck on an island. Using a self-manufactured machine, Markus focuses the sun's rays through a fresnel lens onto a pile of sand. The focal point reaches thousands of degrees, enough to melt the sand and transform it into raw, elemental glass sculptures, one layer at a time.

markuskayser.com

AMAZONIAN KICK
ECUADOR

The health-obsessed, post-cola era demands that our beverages harm our bodies less yet energize us all the same. Tyler Gage, after spending some time in the Ecuadorian Amazon, discovered the local alternative to the better-known guarana or yerba maté: guayusa. From this experience Runa Tea was born, which Tyler co-founded with Dan MacCombie in 2012. The naturally caffeinated energy drink's quest is to yield sustainable livelihoods for the rainforest farmers who supply its ingredients, while providing an all-natural boost to consumers.

runa.org

Solar fares
GLOBAL

Bitcoin has been roundly criticized as a waste of energy, with tens of thousands of computers worldwide crunching meaningless numbers in the hopes of striking gold. SolarCoin, another virtual currency, plans to tap the market to incent solar energy production. Some computation power is needed to keep transactions flowing, but most of the coins will be distributed gratis to anyone who can prove that they generated solar electricity.

Power plant
USA

The murky and mysterious field of synthetic biology—or genetically modifying the living world—comes with its detractors. It could also come with an all-natural flashlight. That's the goal of the Glowing Plant team, a small group of biochemists, entrepreneurs, and genetic hobbyists who developed an auto-luminescent (self-lighting) houseplant. Working from a converted shipping container in San Francisco, they designed a synthetic DNA sequence that mimics the glow of fireflies and bioluminescent marine life. The sequence gets inserted into plant seeds via a "gene gun." Once potted and watered, the plants glow bright enough to replace a reading lamp or light up a dark path. The team raised USD 500,000 on Kickstarter in 2013 and plans to distribute some 600,000 seeds later this year. They aim to light up the imagination, too: the DNA designs and seeds are open-source to encourage people to hack their own glowing plants into new growth. —Bayla Metzger

Sophie Alda

glowingplant.com

19

Neurohacks

UK

Smart drugs are out; DIY neuroenhancers are in. When it comes to brain boosting, head to the community-run London Hackspace for neuron-breaking technology. A team has developed a new method, named transcranial direct current stimulation (tDCS), which applies a small electrical current to your head to stimulate certain areas of the brain. The simple equipment includes two wires, one red and one blue, snaking from a black box with an LED and a red button. On the end of the red wire is an anode; on the end of the blue, a cathode. Two small sponge pads hug the copper electrodes. Soaked in saltwater before fastening to the cranium, the pads are hugged in place by a sweatband. Electric-chair

similarities aside, members claim that tDCS effects bear similarity to Modafinil, a narcolepsy drug that induces alertness. Skepticism hovers around those willing to give it a go, but rumors of complications don't seem to deter newcomers from jolting their brain to the next level.

london.hackspace.org.uk

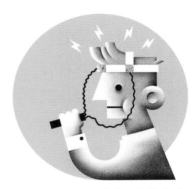

Andrew Colin Beck

Eli Duke

buswk.co/lrFIDPq

 20

SUBURBAN SURVIVALIST

USA

Robin Speronis is something of a rebel in the strip-mall-laden retiree haven of Cape Coral, Florida—though with a cause. Speronis is a suburban survivalist, powering up and washing off without paying a dime to the municipal utilities. Her minimal electricity comes via long wires running from a small solar charger perched on a windowsill; a propane lantern dangling from an overhead light fixture does the night shift. Outside, two squat 200-liter cisterns collect rainwater for bathing, drinking, and toilet flushing, while a solar-heated camp shower keeps bath time toasty. To Cape Coral officials, it's an insurrection. Over the last year, they've tried to kick her out for violating various household codes and ordinances. She spent a month in jail this spring after the city got creative and accused her of animal abuse (the charges were dropped in June). Now she's back at the house, her off-grid rebellion at full steam ahead.

mkshft.org

Want more Makeshift? Our contributors are in the world's bazaars, foundries, and cyber cafes uncovering creative solutions, and we're delivering them to you wherever you are.

Makeshift Online
DIGITAL SUBSCRIPTIONS
ON ANY DEVICE

On Air
VIDEO FEATURES
OF MAKERS

On Assignment
BLOGGING FROM
THE FIELD

From the Makery
WEEKLY EMAILS OF
CREATIVE INSPIRATION

SHOW US YOUR #HIDDENCREATIVITY
@MKSHFTMAG

IN PARTNERSHIP WITH

POWERING UP
ISSUE

NUMBER 10

THIS JUICE IS A STEAL—CLEVER
ENERGY HACKS

BLACK GOLD MARKET
INDONESIA
022

BRAIN WAVES
UNITED STATES
062

STREETSIDE SHOCKS
MEXICO
090

9 780985 036775

Makeshift

A FIELD GUIDE TO HIDDEN CREATIVITY

POWERING UP ISSUE
MAKESHIFT

"The smell of heavy in the a

oil hangs

r."

One farmer's free invention could produce India's calories using a tiny fraction of the water
—One-Liter Farming

Sundaram Verma says that to nourish each plant in the sun-scorched fields of India's Rajasthan state, farmers have to pour out 20 liters of water, on multiple occasions—a hot commodity in drought years. What if, he proposed, the same seedling only needed a single liter of water to survive?

That's the aim of Sundaram's farming technique, an innovation he has tweaked and tinkered with over the last decade. While he's shown it can work on trees burned for biofuel and fed to cattle, he's hoping to prove it out on calorie-rich food crops, oilseeds, and grains, especially as the region grapples with its climate.

I reach Sundaram's home in Danta, a small village-district, after a six-hour drive from Delhi, passing through scruffy terrain sprinkled with signs of modernity. A handful of cars, computers in shops, ubiquitous mobile phones. His son guides me back to the small study where Sundaram awaits.

Reclining in his chair, Sundaram outlines the main idea behind his technique. It does rain in Danta but only during the monsoon season. Unlike others in his region, Sundaram prepares his field in such a way that the ground retains as much monsoon rain as possible, reducing the need to irrigate crops in drier months. "This is where the magic lies," he says.

Out in the fields of Danta, Sundaram shows me his method in action. He leads me to a patch where he's conducting a pilot project for India's Oil and Natural Gas Corporation. It boasts about 500 trees, whose trunks will become wood chips for biofuels and whose dark green leaves will feed the local livestock. He singles out a plant that is dry and leafless on top, a victim of the harsh winds of winter. Then he points to its roots, which are still strong—proof that the plant is well-nourished and healthy enough to bounce back.

Sundaram says he first stumbled onto his one-liter method about 15 years ago, when he was studying dryland farming at the Indian Agriculture Research Institute in New Delhi. After over-tilling the soil near a freshly planted sap-

ling, he realized he had broken the tiny natural air pathways that guide groundwater through the soil, called capillaries. And over the next few months, he couldn't find time to water the tree. To Sundaram's surprise, the plant continued to grow on its own. This led him through a round of experiments that refined his technique.

The first step, he explains, is for farmers to level their fields before the monsoon begins in July. After the first week of rain, farmers deeply plow the field to yank out weeds and allow water to seep into the ground. The process also

Sundaram stands with his one-liter trees in rural Rajasthan.

breaks up capillaries, so that groundwater can't rise to the surface and evaporate. In September, before the last rain of the season, farmers plow the land again. This breaks the capillaries on top but leaves the lower-level tubes intact, keeping a layer of water close to the roots.

Sundaram says farmers usually level and plow the field just once, causing the monsoon rains to wash away the topsoil, rather than replenish the ground. Farmers thus have to irrigate the fields frequently and use more water.

Under Sundaram's method, once the fields are readied before the monsoon, farmers next plant tree saplings into deep pits, with the roots at least 20 centimeters below the surface. Soil is piled on, with a bit of space left empty for watering. In the final step, farmers water the saplings with one liter of water—just one time—and leave the plant to grow without any further

**FARMING
FOR HONEY**
Each year, Anil Gupta takes a week to walk 125 kilometers through India's countryside in search of creativity. In this *shodh yatra*, or journey of exploration, he sources this new knowledge from enterprising farmers and cross-pollinates among others he finds along the way. This is the purpose of his organization, the Honey Bee Network— to support local knowledge and encourage entrepreneurship. Among the more than a million ideas the network has documented: a bull-powered sprayer for agrochemicals and a compost aerator to convert bio-waste into fertilizer. Pollinate ideas from their database below back to your farm or garden.

sristi.org/hbnew

▶ MAKESHIFT ON AIR
Follow Anil Gupta's shodh yatra at
bit.ly/2pmUcP7

intervention, except for regular weeding. Plants have about an 80 percent chance of surviving, he says, compared to 60 percent with water-intensive conventional methods.

His technique may be novel, but many other farmers out here are also searching for ways to make agriculture an easier and more bountiful pursuit. Take Mansukhbhai Jagani, for instance, who lives in the neighboring state of Gujarat. He's retrofitted a diesel-powered bullet motorcycle into a three-wheeled plow. Late Appachan in southwestern Kerala state created a quicker way to scale betel nut and coconut trees. Two thick rubber bands wrap around a tree trunk and attach to a tiny ladder, which has a foot pedal and a hand grip. By simultaneously stepping and pulling, climbers shimmy up.

So far, Sundaram admits, the allure of less water has not convinced many other farmers to adopt his method. People are skeptical that plants can survive on just a liter of water, and they're reluctant to ditch more familiar techniques.

He's also struggled to find enough funding to test the process out for food crops and at a broader scale. Government programs for rural agricultural innovations are unstable and unpredictable, and officials are no more confident in Sundaram, for now. Villagers have reported to him on various occasions that state farming officials have bribed them to keep an eye on Sundaram; they want to know if he sneaks out at night to water the plants or has any other tricks up his sleeve.

No tricks, Sundaram insists, just a technique so simple it just might work. ⊗

📷 **Observed**

Men load large cows onto a truck at the
weekly cattle market in Birohi, a town close
to the India-Bangladesh border. The larger
cows are often smuggled across the porous
borders by wading through the rivers to be
sold at a profit in Bangladesh.

WORDS
ADAM COHN

INDONESIA

ANNUAL OIL P
940,000 BARRELS

ANNUAL OIL
1.7 MILLION BARRELS

The miners of Wonocolo drill for oil across 4,000 small plots of land
— Black Gold Market

Motorcycles laden with grease-covered jerry cans negotiate narrow, pot-holed roads as they carry oil through the jungle to market. The smell of oil hangs heavy in the air. Scattered among the hills are plots of land cleared of trees and blackened by crude oil. This is Wonocolo, the pockmarked capital of DIY drilling in Indonesia's southeastern province of Cepu.

Felled trees, wire cables, arrays of pulleys, and truck engines are jerry-rigged to create makeshift oil derricks. Crude oil flows down the hills through shallow ditches into pools where it is collected by oil-drenched men and distilled into diesel fuel, which is then driven into town and sold on the black market.

Complex local land ownership has stalled formal oil production here. Some 3,000 landowners hold some 4,000 plots of land below which the petroleum resides, making it nearly impossible for oil conglomerates to ramp up large-scale production (though they do operate oil wells in the vicinity too). In the meantime, entrepreneurs in Cepu have taken on a more artisanal reality—a rugged and unique approach in the modern era.

Disassembled diesel trucks are secured to the ground a short distance from each derrick. Bailers, dropped down the 400-meter wells, are attached by wire cable to the drivetrains of the trucks, and when the operator stomps the gas pedal, the bailer rockets up through the earth, bringing with it a gush of "black gold". Oil drums full of crude are set upon fires lit in holes dug into the hillside, distilling the emulsion into diesel fuel. Every few hours, motorcycles return, pick up the stained jerry cans, and sell the hand-refined oil for a few dollars in nearby markets. ⊗

| MAKING IT | ISSUE 10 | POWERING UP | |
| GLOBAL | NUCLEAR POWER GENERATED 370,000 MW | | NUMBER OF REACTORS 435 IN 31 COUNTRIES |

WORDS
MARIA GALLUCCI

ILLUSTRATION
RONA BINAY

Building a mini nuclear reactor in your home requires only spare parts and basic physics
—DIY Fusion

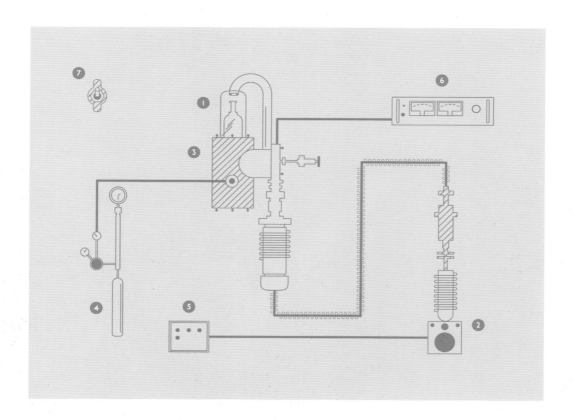

Call it extreme DIY. Across the globe, handfuls of "fusioneers"—engineering hobbyists and amateur physicists—are building nuclear fusion reactors in their basements and backyards. They're driven partly by the thrill of tinkering and partly by the promise of solving one of the world's biggest problems: how to create clean, carbon-free energy on the cheap.

In nuclear fusion, atoms are forced together at high temperatures and pressures, a process that releases energy. According to Fusor.net, the main hub for fusioneers, nearly 60 people have achieved nuclear fusion from a homemade reactor—the youngest of whom is just 14 years old.

Building a tabletop nuclear plant involves lethal electricity voltage levels, explosive gases, and potentially hazardous x-ray exposure. But it doesn't require plutonium or uranium. Here's an abbreviated guide adapted from our friends at Instructables. ⊗

GET A VACUUM CHAMBER

Shop eBay for a spherical vacuum chamber, which pumps out air and other gases to create a low-pressure environment. Or scrounge for parts— including two steel hemispheres, eight-inch rims called "flanges", and bolts—and weld them together using tungsten inert gas.

PREPARE THE VACUUM PUMP

Find a diffusion pump, fill it with low-vapor oil, and connect the pump's inlet to a valve on the vacuum chamber. This will lower the chamber's pressure (making it a stronger vacuum). Then attach the diffusion pump to a mechanical pump, which will remove gas molecules.

BUILD AN INNER GRID

Assemble your electrical wires, preferably ones made of tungsten, since the metal has a high melting point. Attach the wires to a high-voltage (around 40 kilovolts) electrical feedthrough. Don't get zapped.

ASSEMBLE THE DEUTERIUM SYSTEM

Select a fine tank of deuterium from your cellar of dangerous and explosive gases. Attach a high-pressure regulator directly to the tank; this will keep the flow of gas at a safe pressure. Add a needle valve to more precisely regulate the gas flow. Connect this all to the vacuum chamber.

CONFIGURE THE POWER SUPPLY

Snag a high-voltage power supply module on the web. Take the negative voltage output and attach it to the chamber, and throw on a large ballast resistor, which will limit the amount of electrical current flowing through the circuit.

SET UP THE NEUTRON DETECTOR

To prove you've fused atoms, you'll need to detect neutron radiation. The easiest and most accurate way to do this is with a "proportional tube". You can buy ones filled with BF3 or Helium-3 gases and attach a counting device. This will detect electrical pulses each time neutrons pass through the tube. These tubes are extremely expensive, so fusioneers have created their own versions.

LET'S FUSE

Ready? Turn on the mechanical pump and oil diffusion pump, and wait for it to warm up. Throttle the valve that connects the pumps to the vacuum chamber, and gently open the needle valve to the deuterium gas tank. Flip on the power supply. Keep pumping gas and adding pressure until you detect neutron radiation pumping through your tubes. Congratulations! You've just fused.

This guide was adapted from an article on Instructables by christensent

bit.ly/IENOQG

SODABI PRICE	SODABI PROOF
USD 1-2 PER L	90

📷 Observed

Sodabi is a popular alcoholic beverage in Benin, made from sugar cane. Zanzan, a voodoo priest in Ouidah, marinates snakes in sodabi to make a powerful concoction believed to protect the drinker and make him invisible to enemies.

If you need good luck, a nine-tailed lizard at Bangkok's amulet market is said to whip cash into your pocket
—Pocket Protectors

Thailand's highways aren't for timid drivers, with inundated roads, erratic speeders, and a cultural disdain for seat belts taking thousands of lives each year. So when Pitak Veangsima, a marketing executive, careened his Lamborghini off a road at 150 kph in June and smashed into a tree, it seemed as though he would be just one more goner.

Yet while his million-dollar vehicle was split in two, Pitak escaped unscathed: he calmly walked away from the wreckage to call his insurance company. Simple reasoning might posit that Pitak was either the luckiest man alive or the beneficiary of Lamborghini engineers, who some say designed the car to separate into two chunks in such high-impact situations.

Pitak, however, had no doubt about where his good fortune came from. As he saw it, his survival was thanks to protective energies emanating from the prized Buddhist amulet—a simple charm with an image of Buddha—that dangled from his neck at the time of the crash.

In other highly publicized incidents in Thailand, amulets have helped owners dodge bullets and avoid fatal plunges. Millions of Thais, in fact, can reference specific, often unfathomable incidents that prove the power of their amulets. Wearers believe that the small trinkets—ostensibly blessed by Buddhist monks—can generate enough positive energy to bring them everything from good luck and true love to wild sex and hard cash.

A vendor in Bangkok's main amulet market sorts through his wares.

Amulets often bear the
image of religious deities.
In the top-left corner, two
large pieces feature the
elephant-headed Ganesha,
believed to bring wisdom.

The ancient
history of amulets
lies wrapped
in the slew of
intermingling
beliefs—
Hindu, animist,
superstitious, and
Buddhist—that
define Thai culture.

"I swear by them," says Prachat, a customer at Bangkok's main amulet market near Phra Chan Road, who owns more than 300 different objects. "They have helped me in many ways. Some are blessed by monks who are known for being wise, which gives me wisdom. Others are blessed by monks legendary for their generosity and kindness. These help me to care for my family."

At the market, in the historic old city, stallholders lay out a bewildering selection of the energized trinkets. Amulets come in many styles and shapes and are made of metal, wood, bone, or plaster. They can also include colored dust from a temple's bricks, human hair, and even droplets of blood.

Many of the palm-sized amulets depict Buddha or a senior monk in bas-relief. These are known as *Phra Kreuang*. Other versions are more bizarre. A macabre two-headed zombie baby is said to be a guardian angel, while one with the antlers of a muntjac deer is meant to bring prosperity. Nine-tailed lizards are added to whip more money into the pocket of the owner.

The most expensive amulets are carefully placed in separate velvet-lined compartments in cabinets made from golden teak wood. Less valuable amulets are placed in more modest cabinets, while the cheapest items are carried to the market in plastic shopping bags and set out roughly on ramshackle tables. Salesmen shuffle the mass-produced items around based on cycles of popularity, though antique amulets and ones blessed by recognized master monks never go out of style.

The showcasing techniques do not necessarily reflect the spiritual power of the amulets, however; the vendors are simply trying to lure buyers to pricier trinkets. Many shoppers know this, and when they buy expensive amulets, it's less to take on extra powers than to display their status—like a flashy sports car or designer handbag.

Everyday shoppers can pick up amulets at the market—as well as in temples and department stores across the country—for as little as 10 baht (USD 0.30). High-end versions, prized by elite businessmen, decorated policemen and soldiers, regularly sell for over 3 million baht (USD 100,000). Pitak's amulet, blessed by Luang Phor Sodh, one of Thailand's most revered monks, costs roughly this much. The most elite versions are ones blessed by Somdej Toh, another prominent monk from the 19th century.

The ancient history of amulets lies wrapped in the slew of intermingling beliefs—Hindu, animist, superstitious, and Buddhist—that define Thai culture. But as Thailand modernizes, its amulet industry is becoming increasingly commercialized. In the past, monks made just a few precious amulets. Today, amulets are mass-produced by more than a dozen domestic companies. Once a new design is finalized, batches are sent to selected temples to be blessed, resulting in lucrative tax-free profits for many monks.

All told, Thailand's amulet industry is worth over a hundred million dollars a year. Beyond Thailand, the trinkets are extremely popular as a mystical source of energy and a fashionable accessory in other Asian markets and in Western countries.

Some Thai people complain that the amulet trend is just another example of the blatant monetization of Thai-style Buddhism. Others think the items are merely a superstitious scam.

"I think they are meaningless now," says Apple Tangsinpoonchai, a 29-year-old Bangkok journalist. "Before, they signified something ceremonial and holy, as they were originally used as decorations in temples or good luck charms. Nowadays, they are as much of a fashion statement as anything else."

Back at the Bangkok market, however, belief in the amulet's transformative energy still thrives. Customers browsing the pieces span young

ANCIENT PROTECTION

Amulets have been protecting their owners from harm since ancient times. The word "amulet" comes from the Latin *amuletum*, which means "an object that protects a person from trouble". The earliest mention of the word is in *Natural History*, the early encyclopedia published around 77 AD by Roman philosopher Pliny the Elder.

Fascinus
One of many amulets employed by ancient Romans to invoke the powers of an associated god—in this case, a phallus to protect women and children from envy, or "the evil eye".

Mezuzah
A piece of parchment inscribed with specific Hebrew verses from the Torah, which acts as a symbol of God's watch upon the homes of Jews.

Scarab
Symbolizing rebirth and sunrise, ancient Egyptians used scarab amulets during funerary rites—for example, a heart scarab to protect the heart from speaking out against the deceased.

Inspecting pieces at a stall in Bangkok's amulet market.

and old, poor and affluent. Patchwipa Malika, a 30-year-old who works in the medical industry, is searching for a piece blessed by the monk Luang Phor Thod believed to protect travelers on their journeys.

She just landed a lucrative new job, but she doesn't chalk her good fortune up to serendipity or skill. Instead, she attributes her employment to the mysterious powers of the collection of amulets she keeps in the glove box of her BMW convertible.

"I know it maybe sounds crazy to some foreigners, but I am a Buddhist and I believe in their energies," she says of the amulets. "I hadn't even put my resume online yet somehow, someone from Holland got hold of my details and gave me this opportunity. I know that, to a certain degree, you make your own luck in life, but I am very much of the belief that [the amulets] have aided me and protected me." ⊗

Makeshift is made
possible by

How does a many-to-many
approach empower organizations
and communities?
—Learn more at opnbx.com

Now nighttime can also
mean match time
—Innovative and renewable
energy solutions will help bring
reliable electricity to Africa

First night
victory

HAN

A coat is no longer a coat, but rather
the specific details of that quote
—Modernized classics

SVA★NYC
DSI
Design for Social Innovation

Design for Social Innovation at SVA
is the first MFA program for creative leaders
who will use design to help enterprise,
humanity and the planet thrive
— Apply

DSI.SVA.EDU

AUTODESK.

Creating local solutions
to global energy challenges?
—Share your sustainable energy projects
with the Instructables community

INSTRUCTABLES.COM

FATH✷M
WAY TO GO

Insider knowledge. The world's
best places. Inspired travelers
—Explore the world with Fathom

FATHOMAWAY.COM

"Nobody can s
tapping into th
taking electric

top us from
ne grid and
ity."

One-fifth of Venezuelan fuel exports leave the country illegally —Combustible Contraband

Gregorio speeds his Ford 350 at 100 kilometers per hour down an unpaved road through the bushes. His truck and two others behind him are each smuggling 100 barrels of Venezuelan gasoline into Colombia— their destination a small ranch near Santa Rosa, in the Caribbean state of La Guajira. Gregorio catches word that the Venezuelan military is closing in on his caravan. "The guards had closed several back roads, so we had to invent new ones," he recounts from an open café in Maicao, Colombia, the main city in the area.

For a year and a half, Gregorio has smuggled gas through clandestine routes along the inhospitable frontier, marked only by the desolated ranches of indigenous Wayúu people. He can earn up to 20,000 bolívares a week (USD 300 officially speaking, or USD 2,000 on the black market; Venezuela has several exchange rates).

His operation is bolstered by this simple fact: in Venezuela, a liter of gasoline officially costs a cent and a half, thanks to heavy government subsidies that make it the cheapest gas in the world. But at black market prices, a liter costs next to nothing: a tenth of a cent. In neighboring Colombia, by contrast, gasoline runs USD 1.20 per liter.

Many residents along the 2,219-kilometer Venezuela-Colombia border have turned to fuel smuggling to earn a living over the past decade. They siphon off fuel and pour it into tanks, plastic drums, and bottles, which are then slipped under car hoods, tucked above tires, and hidden behind car seats. It's a predictably dirty job. Gas often leaks from plastic jerry cans and into local creeks. Smugglers can develop throat and stomach illnesses because they use a straw-like hose to shuffle fuel from container to container, and they sometimes swallow it. Charred remains of vehicles litter the sides of roads, oil drums visible from the back seat or trunk.

Still, the illicit industry "provides a profit that you can't even get in the drug trade", José Guerra, a Caracas-based economist, says. "Venezuela's economic policies in the last 15 years have created such distortions."

Ricardo, a young man in San Antonio, a border town in southwest Venezuela, says he earns around 5,000 bolívares (USD 800, officially) a week by lugging a 19-liter tank of gas into Colombia on his Yamaha 250 motorcycle. That's about five times what he could make as a bike messenger at home. Nearly every day, he rides the two kilometers into Cúcuta, the main city in northeastern Colombia, and his haul can fetch around USD 8 for the whole tank.

Altogether, around 25,000 barrels, or nearly 4 million liters, of Venezuelan gasoline are smuggled every day into Colombia, Brazil, and the English Caribbean, officials estimate.

Rafael Ramírez, Venezuela's former energy minister, figures that the country loses about USD 1.5 billion in annual oil revenues because of the illicit trade. As President Nicolás Maduro struggles to adopt a policy to fix the gas price problem, he is stepping up enforcement. Maduro recently ordered 17,000 troops to police the border with Colombia, and frontier entrances are now closed at night.

Altogether, around 25,000 barrels, or nearly 4 million liters, of Venezuelan gasoline are smuggled every day into Colombia, Brazil, and the English Caribbean.

Each day, thousands of barrels of illicit fuel sneak through this border checkpoint between San Antonio, Venezuela, and Cúcuta, Colombia.

Like Gregorio, Ricardo is finding ways around the human roadblocks. "At the border checkpoint, the National Guard will take away half of my gas tank," he says. "I have to come up with another route to cross, one where a guard will take USD 50 or 100 to let me through."

Danilo, who rides in Gregorio's truck, similarly carries a stack of cash to grease palms along the way. The crew is often intercepted by *civiles* demanding bribes from 1,000 bolívares (USD 12) on up. Civiles include military and police from both countries, as well as armed men from the left-wing guerrilla group FARC, paramilitary gangs, or Wayúu people who control certain swathes of land.

If and when the smugglers get through, their fuel finds its way to *pimpineros* (roadside vendors) like Edgar Medina. A 17-year-old dressed in shorts, a T-shirt, and sandals, he parks himself near the entrance to Cúcuta, an astoundingly toasty city. He sells around 40 *pimpinas* (23-liter jerry cans) a day along the road that connects to San Antonio in Venezuela.

"Up until July, I was buying pimpinas at 22,000 Colombian pesos (USD 11) and selling for 28,000 pesos," he says from an improvised hut made from logs, scrap plastic, and zinc. Since Venezuela's National Guard has started cracking down, however, less fuel is pouring into Colombia, enabling him to raise his prices. He now buys at 28,000 pesos and sells for 33,000 pesos.

> "I have to come up with another route to cross, one where a guard will take USD 50 or 100 to let me through."

The many streetside iterations of fuel arbitrage throughout the Venezuela-Colombia border region.

GREASY ROUTES

Traffickers funnel 4 million liters of fuel out of
Venezuela each day. Where does it go?

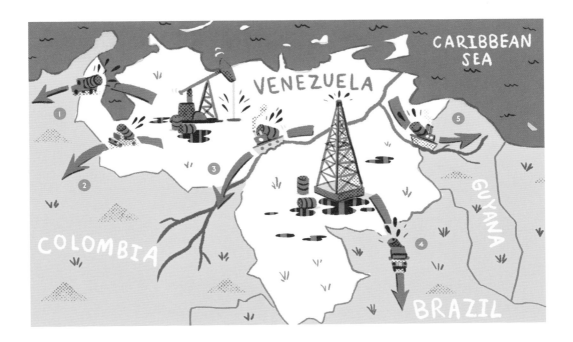

1. Gregorio smuggles
fuel from Venezuela
to Santa Rosa, in
the Caribbean
state of La Guajira,
Colombia.

2. Ricardo's route
takes him from
San Antonio,
Venezuela to
Cúcuta, Colombia.
Edgar runs a fuel
stand on the same
road near Cúcuta.

3. Fuel is also
smuggled into
Colombia via three
rivers near the
borders: Rio
Arauca, Rio Meta,
and Rio Orinoco.

4. Venezuela's
southern border
is another key
smuggling zone.
One reported route
runs from the town
of Elena de Uairén
to Pacaraima, Brazil,
in the Amazon basin.

5. Guyana is also
a market for
illicit Venezuelan
gasoline. The fuel
has reportedly
shown up on
the coast of the
Essequibo River,
near Georgetown.

Even at the higher cost, a car owner in eastern Colombia can still get gas for half or one-third of the price he would pay at an actual service station. About 15 percent of all gas used in Colombia is contraband, customs officials estimate.

How the fuel gets from the smuggler to the pimpinero is somewhat murky. Edgar says he gets his supplies from a wholesaler, who delivers a batch of pimpinas by van. "I just know him as Alfonso, and I don't ask him many questions," he says. In Maicao, up to 200 enclosed lots receive gasoline drums and send them to unregulated selling stations. Colombian and Venezuelan media both report that paramilitary troops—now "demobilized" from Colombia's armed conflict with FARC—are the main shareholders in this illegal fuel trade.

Fuel smuggling in the region could not thrive without the complicity of formal gas distributors in Venezuela, who are part of Venezuela's petroleum monopoly PDVSA. Nor could it succeed without the secret support of the country's armed forces, according to civilian opposition figures. In late August, 21 military officials were taken to court because, while their colleagues were closing off some of the 400 informal roads crossing through the Venezuela-Colombia border, the officials were opening up new routes for the smugglers and their trucks.

Reflecting on what he does, Danilo maintains that the frontier has been a source of livelihood for generations. "Folks have always profited from the border trade. Long ago, it was the other way around—people smuggling from Colombia to Venezuela. It's always been a way to make money." ⊗

Several names in this story are pseudonyms given to the writer due to security concerns.

(▶) MAKESHIFT ON AIR
Check mkshft.org for our upcoming video featuring Venezuela's fuel smugglers.

⌖ Observed

Boys carry empty 240-liter barrels to a
warehouse near the Togo-Benin border
where tens of thousands of liters of illegal
fuel are stored. A smuggler, who declined
to give his name, says the illegal fuel trade
provides valuable jobs in a country where
most earn less than USD I per day.

To beat Shanghai's traffic and urban sprawl, cargo drivers fuse together e-bikes and trikes
—Hybrid Haulers

From the edge of the sidewalk, I jump back at the last second. Alerted by a frenetic mechanical whine bursting over the din of traffic, I narrowly missed a severe clipping by a three-wheeled vehicle careening past me before ducking down the nearest alleyway.

A typical Shanghai rush hour, the streets clog with German luxury cars, cargo trucks, and bicycles, resembling the increasingly generic feel of the modern-day global metropolis. Luckily for me, this particular buzzing—one of the unique members of urban China's transport fleet—stands out from the crowd.

The renegade cargo tricycle is powered by both human legs and batteries, and it carts everything from furniture and fruit to construction materials and—on days of lax traffic enforcement—even laborers. Hybrid haulers

A modified, front-wheel drive hauler sits ready to rip (left), courtesy of its hacked-together electrical box (above).

can carry a considerable load for their humble size. The large ones, up to 450 kilograms, need more and newer batteries; smaller haulers, less. Unmatched in their ability to rapidly traverse narrow spaces, they dominate the alleys (and sidewalks, when necessary) that run parallel to Shanghai's runway-sized avenues.

The renegade cargo tricycle is powered by both human legs and batteries, and it carts everything from furniture and fruit to construction materials and—on days of lax traffic regulations—even laborers.

Shanghai has long hosted conventional tricycles that carve through traffic over half-built infrastructure in the quest to transport the goods and services that keep the city sprinting forward. But as Shanghai expands and becomes increasingly congested, more materials must be transported over greater distances. For the delivery workers who can't afford cargo vans (and accompanying driver's testing and licensing fees), hybrid tricycles fill a critical gap.

The haulers were largely born out of China's growing love affair with the e-bike. With over 200 million pure-electric or hybrid bicycles on Chinese roads, more than one in 10 people across the nation (or roughly 112 million) have bought such a bike—often for as little as 2,000 yuan (USD 320). E-bike proliferation has created a thriving market for spare parts, such as batteries and electric drive wheels, making it relatively cheap and increasingly popular to upgrade a man-powered three-wheeler into a hybrid hauler.

Bicycle fixers typically electrify tricycles in small shops and junkyards outside central Shanghai. At one such shop, the air heavy with the smell of lubricating grease and screeches of a circular saw, I sat and spoke with Peng, the owner, as he huddled over a multicolored bird's nest of wires, deftly untangling them and occasionally glancing down to check his work. He says that among police officers and car drivers, "there's prejudice against these vehicles. People think they're too uncivilized."

While Peng originally moved out to this remote suburb seeking cheaper space for his workshop, this neighborhood is now one of the few places where the hybrid cargo tricycles he works on can travel freely. Because of the perceived recklessness of their drivers, hybrid tricycles are banned from the city center. Although the tricycle riders can usually find work on far-flung construction sites on the city's periphery, when drivers do venture downtown, they return to this suburban shop with tales of harassment or steep fines at the hands of the traffic police.

BUILD YOUR OWN HAULER

1. Pick up components from a scrapped or stolen e-bike. You'll need an e-bike drive-wheel, which spins when given an electrical charge; an accelerator/controller from the handlebar, which controls the flow of electricity from the battery to the drive wheel; and an ignition switch, which uses a key to flip on the motor.

2. Find and connect a battery. Low-quality, refurbished versions are cheap and widely available thanks to the e-bike boom.

Installing multiple batteries grants additional range, but it requires a voltage regulator to manage the power. It also means greater weight and less cargo space. A heavy-gauge chain and padlock will protect from theft.

3. Find a welder or bicycle shop to wire together your components.

4. Customize it by adding parts like a cargo box, battery weather protectors, or horns and headlights for safety.

One of many
applications of the multi-
purpose e-bikes, this
one's for the hungry.

Examine any 10 haulers and you'll find 10
unique vehicles—each as individual as the
craftsmen who made them. If you don't mind
a perpetual forward lean, an unmodified cargo
tricycle's larger front wheel can be swapped out
directly for an e-bike's smaller, battery-pow-
ered drive wheel assembly. Or, rather than
use the e-bike wheel like a traditional tire that
touches the ground, mechanics also mount it to
the tricycle's rear axle. When electricity turns
the wheel, the rear axle spins and pushes the
vehicle forward.

Regardless of the configuration, stay alert
if you ever find yourself wandering Shanghai
streets—or sidewalks. If you focus too much on
dodging cars, buses, and bicycles, you may miss
the telltale whine of the overtaxed hybrids until
they're suddenly on top of you. ⊗

Twice a day in Fairfield, 2,000 visitors from 50 countries congregate to meditate
—Brain Waves

Barry Miller has meditated eight hours a day for the past seven years. He doesn't live in Tibet or India or even Berkeley, California. Barry is just a typical resident of Fairfield, known in some circles as North America's mecca of enlightenment.

Surrounded by cornfields and the farmland typical of the rural Midwest, Fairfield is a city of just under 10,000 people in southeastern Iowa. It is also home to the Maharishi University of Management, which offers intensive meditation training and attracts students from around the world interested in tapping into this area's own brand of energy.

While not everyone in Fairfield meditates, the majority do. Barry's wife, Jennifer, a 66-year-old web developer, says their group of friends is a mix. "Out of 18 families, four of them do not meditate and the others do." Jennifer has been meditating for 43 years. For a period of time, she was also meditating for six to eight hours a day, but now, because of work, she does a session in the morning and then again in the evening, each lasting about an hour and a half.

TM is like you have a cell phone, and someone gives you the charger.

The kind of meditation Fairfield's inhabitants practice is called Transcendental Meditation (TM). It involves the use of a sound or mantra and, because it's standardized and replicable, it has attracted the attention of neuroscientists and researchers across the country.

BALANCED SCIENCE

What is it about meditation that provides the positive charge? Or is it even there at all? In addition to the increased cortical thickness that Dr. Lazar described, a study she conducted with non-meditators who participated in an eight-week meditation program demonstrated the following results:

(A) Noticeable growth in the hippocampus, which is important for emotional regulation

(B) Decrease in the size of the amygdala, which controls the body's "fight or flight" reflex

(C) Lower cortisol levels, which indicates reduced stress

According to the Transcendental Meditation website, the practice "allows your mind to easily settle inward, through quieter levels of thought, until you experience the most silent and peaceful level of your own awareness—pure consciousness." If you're skeptical, you're not alone. Meditation was long dismissed by scientific researchers. Recently though, a number of leading neuroscientists have examined the effects of meditation and found surprising results of which parts of the brain it may tap.

Harvard neuroscientist Dr. Sara Lazar has conducted extensive research on the physical effects of various types of meditation on the brain. Her findings provide some clues as to how meditation may actually work. Sara found that parts of the frontal cortex, an area of the brain used in decision-making and cognitive processing, are larger in meditators. She writes that it's well-known "that this part of the brain normally decreases in thickness as we age. Interestingly, when we plotted each person's

Channeling energy from
wherever there is enough
space for a small mat.

cortical thickness in this region against his or her age, the graph suggested that meditation might help to slow down or even prevent this normal age-related decline in thickness."

Barry is retired, and so his schedule is more flexible and can accommodate a full day of meditation. Hard to imagine? Many fellow Fairfield residents have moved there explicitly for the intensive meditation and community the university and town provide. Barry worked his way through college doing manual labor at construction sites. After hours of hauling around wheelbarrows of concrete, he'd come home exhausted and fall asleep on the couch. But according to Jennifer, "After he learned TM, he would come home and he'd meditate, and then he's ready to go. He'd have a full evening of activity in front of him."

Barry's not the only practitioner who finds that meditation recharges his batteries. Numerous celebrities have embraced the technique, among them Russell Simmons and Ellen DeGeneres. The filmmaker David Lynch even started a foundation to promote TM worldwide. At a fundraising gala for the foundation, comedian Jerry Seinfeld described the high stress of creating and starring in a hit sitcom and said that he attributed his success to regular meditation: "TM is like you have a cell phone and someone gives you the charger."

Beyond the celebrity endorsements, other studies suggest other powers at work in the TM practice. A now-famous focused action of TM practitioners in Washington, DC, meditating for peace in the summer of 1993, saw a corresponding drop in violent crimes of 23 percent during the period of meditation. The term "Maharishi Effect" describes the intangible product that results from concentrated pockets of meditation, and is believed by some to explain the Washington study, or the peacefulness of places like Fairfield. More recent studies have shown to reduce youth violence and improve wellbeing in schools when students are exposed to meditation—further suggesting that the correct frequencies are being tapped.

For Jennifer, the results of 40 years of practice have been more personal. "I've continued all this time without really noticing big, huge flashy things. But what I have noticed is that I have this kind of inner calm." Jerry Seinfeld agrees. "You know that tremendous feeling of power when your phone is fully charged?" he asks the fundraiser crowd. "Someone calls and you go, 'I want to hear *every* detail of this story! I am loaded with juice.' That's what TM is like."

If true, it would seem to follow that Kramer was the sitcom's most devout practitioner of the bunch. ⊗

Observed

The CaiRollers settle into a new practice site after months of searching. The roller derby team—established by American expats to empower women in a restrictive culture—thrashes through each raucous, full-contact match.

	WORDS & PHOTOS **RAPHAEL WRIGHT**
DETROIT — US	UNPAID ENERGY & WATER BILLS **USD 53 MILLION**
	DEBT AT CITY BANKRUPTCY **USD 18 BILLION**

A tenth of Detroit's residents obtain their electricity illegally
—Grid Grab

Clyde "Chuck" Jones is an off-the-books handyman living and working in Detroit's east side. On a recent balmy weekday, he picked up a few odd jobs around the block: USD 15 to mow his neighbor's lawn, a few dollars more to fix a car up the street. But his last job for the day—and his favorite—will pay a pretty USD 200. For this he'll have to illegally hook up a home to the city's electricity grid.

Chuck is part of Detroit's brigade of energy pirates helping an estimated 70,000 residents—about 10 percent of the population—to illicitly connect to municipal utility lines. The numbers are only rising as the bankrupt city struggles to turn its economy around.

"I've turned on hundreds of homes, even turning the power on at a nightclub," Chuck says as he prepares to perform his sunset gig. His client this evening is a homeowner converting the place into a rental property. "Everybody

wants a deal. If you could get away with it, I guarantee you'd do it too."

Detroit's illegal energy customers aren't just residents who can't afford to keep the lights on, though many of them are. Chuck says he's also serviced upper-class customers and small business owners. For Detroiters, finding an energy

Chuck is part of Detroit's brigade of energy pirates helping an estimated 70,000 residents—about 10 percent of the population—to connect to municipal utility lines.

pirate is fairly easy; in most cases, it only takes one phone call. Using simple tools like wire cutters and pliers, they rig power panels to the backs of people's homes. Or they'll climb a light pole to fudge with the wires and send power to homes without municipal services.

The energy savings for customers, however, can come at a high cost for pirates. Some say they've been electrocuted multiple times while hacking the grid. Earlier this year, one man set himself on fire while working on wires from a tree. "If you don't have experience or knowledge in this field, you can botch a lot of jobs or kill yourself," Chuck cautions. Faulty work has also damaged buildings and electrical infrastructure around the city.

One of many properties looking for tenants amidst Detroit's struggling economy.

Still, many energy bandits believe the risks are worth—and justified in—taking. Unemployment here is more than twice the national average, and Detroit has been in a recession for decades. These electricians are mostly poor and struggling to survive, like Chuck is. "There ain't no jobs here, so a lot of us turned to the underground economy to make ends meet," he says.

Now in his mid-50s, Chuck remembers the tail end of the east side's glory days. In the 1950s, his father worked at the Ford Motor plant right up the street, and his mother worked as a seamstress at a local dry cleaner. But racial tensions and a sluggish economy sent residents flocking to the suburbs, turning much of downtown Detroit into a ghost town.

Crime rates spiked during the 1980s crack epidemic, and rounds of mass layoffs at the major automakers later followed. Now the only signs of a formal economy around Chuck's Mack Avenue neighborhood are liquor stores and gas stations. "Things are nowhere near what they used to be," he says.

Chuck initially honed his electrical skills as a formal contractor. Then, accused of committing an armed robbery, he spent the next six years in prison. After his release, it was virtually impossible for him to find stable work. So he took his knowledge of electrical technique to the streets.

He has various methods for doing the deed. He's used jumper cables—typically meant for charging car batteries—to siphon current from electrical transmitters that sit atop wooden power poles. The cables then send power down to homes and office buildings. He's also fixed the power panels on the back of houses with household scissors. To hook up his own home, he modified a small rectangular backup generator and attached it directly to a power pole.

His large four-bedroom house has faulty electrical circuits, a refrigerator that's barely functioning, and a battered roof that leaks furi-

ously on rainy days. To power up the place, he hooked the generator to a wire, connected on the other end to a breaker, which sends current to homes and buildings within a particular slice of the grid. A second wire, which would normally be connected to the pole, is instead tied to the generator on one end and to his house on the other. This hacked-up system in turn keeps Chuck's lights on—not surprisingly, free of charge.

Chuck says he used to fill up the generator with gasoline before installing it on the pole, but the mix of fuel and high voltage entering and exiting the device would cause it to explode. Now, he keeps it empty and uses only the wires to power it up.

In recent months, Detroit's energy pirates have come under increasing scrutiny from utility company DTE Energy and the city's police department. Together they're studying the pirates' networks, their hotspots, and the techniques they use to steal electricity, with the hopes of creating counter-plans to stop the hacking. In the case of tap water, municipal workers have started filling up some people's intakes with rocks so they can't illegally connect to the pipes.

"If you don't have experience or knowledge in the field, you can botch a lot of jobs or kill yourself."

"They think they can operate (with) impunity," the RAND research organization has said about pirates in Detroit and around the world. As global demand surges for illegal services, the thieves have become "more sophisticated, more brash".

Chuck says the city's efforts are a waste of time. "Nobody can stop us from tapping into the grid and taking electricity." He reasons that pirates are creative enough to work around the utility's attempts to thwart them. Even if companies and city departments change how services are distributed, the pirates will find a way to create opportunities to earn a living, he says.

With his evening job over and work day winding down, Chuck is ecstatic that he finished the high-paying gig in less than 20 minutes. "200 dollars to do nothing," he says as we walk toward his home. As he vigorously rubs his dog's head, Chuck says, "I will be able to buy food and a tarp for my roof." ⊗

The discreet work of a pirate.

WORDS
JUSTIN LEVINSON & MARIA GALLUCCI

ILLUSTRATION
SOPHIE ALDA

GLOBAL

WORLD ELECTRICITY GENERATION
21 TRILLION KWH

ANNUAL COST OF ELECTRICITY LOSS
USD 202 BILLION

Pry it, hack it, tap it, cut it—the world's electricity systems are open for the taking
—Joule Thieves

Power theft is prone to happen in any place with overhead cables and a tall wooden pole. Detroit has its pirates, Brazil has its *gatos*, and Uganda has social networks that outsmart the authorities. Energy thieves steal because they have to or just because they can. Makeshift uncovered a few of the ways hackers get their joule fix. ⊗

LIGHT POLES
New York City

Hip-hop's history is rooted in street lights and lamp posts. In the 1970s, DJ Kool Herc, hailed as the world's first hip-hop DJ, powered his turntables and amps from the base of a pole. He got the idea from construction crews, who, along with homeless people, had been guzzling kilowatts this way since forever. In the latest incarnation, smartphone users are prying open the poles' flap doors to charge their devices. Some DIYers have risked hard-wiring outlets, but word on the street is some posts have them built in.

SMART METERS
San Juan

Across the global grid, digital electricity meters are ousting analog boxes. While boosting efficiency, they're vulnerable to hacking, prompting fears from home robberies to terrorist attacks on the grid. In Puerto Rico, a utility lost hundreds of millions of dollars after enterprising criminals figured out how to reprogram meters to avoid payment and offered their services to cut consumers' bills. Pairing a laptop to a homemade infrared link, the thieves stopped the meter from recording energy usage without cracking the physical case.

BYPASS
Kampala

Here in Uganda's capital, residents have found at least eight ways to "bypass" the city's meters and power lines. The most common is the "diagonal", which reattaches electrical contacts so current doesn't flow through the meter. Another, called a "ghost meter", moves meters to parts of the city where their activity won't be tracked. The work is backed by "social warning systems" in which community members call the leader of an illegal electrician network to warn of surprise meter audits or police patrols in the area.
—**Jeffrey K. Hall**

GATOS
Rio de Janeiro

Residents in Rio's jam-packed *favelas* and formal "asphalt" neighborhoods connect to the grid with *gatos*, or "cats", which illegally supply nearly three-fourths of electricity in some areas. Cables are attached directly to transmission lines—a sometimes fatal practice—and a wire is connected to the outside of the meter, which stops it from registering consumption. A hole is then drilled into the meter display, and another wire manipulates the hardware. Finally, the teeth of the meter's gears are broken so the display can't rotate forward.
—**Russ Slater**

BAT HOOKS
Washington, DC

If Batman slung his wing-shaped hook over a power line, he'd burn to a crisp. But the US Air Force version of the bat hook is meant for high voltages, allowing soldiers to siphon off electricity and recharge equipment in the field. A blade on the headpiece pierces the wire insulation, allowing the device's innards to make contact with bare cable. Electricity then funnels down a wire to the load. Civilians worldwide have been building scrappier versions of the bat hook for decades, slinging a metal hook over the cable, leading into their homes.

OBSERVED

QAMISHLI
— SYRIA

ISSUE 10

PHOTO
CENGIZ YAR

POWERING UP

AVG AUGUST HIGH TEMPERATURE
40 °C

AVG AUGUST PRECIPITATION
0.3 MM

Observed

Two young men check their mobile
phones before going to sleep on the roof
of their parents' house on the outskirts
of Qamishli. Frequent power outages and
fuel shortages make for uncomfortable
indoor sleeping on warm nights.

⚡

RUSSIA

WORDS
MARIA GALLUCCI

ANNUAL ELECTRICITY USAGE
850 BILLION KWH

ENERGY LOSS IN TRANSMISSION
10%

Two inventors have revived Nikola Tesla's vision of wireless energy for the entire planet
—Tesla's Tower

What if electricity could travel the way data does, unburdened by clunky infrastructure as current flows wirelessly? That was inventor Nikola Tesla's vision more than a century ago. With his Wardenclyffe tower, he set out to use the Earth's surface in lieu of cables to transmit energy from power plant to light bulb. Although he demonstrated it could work, he eventually shut the project down, believing the world wasn't yet ready for such transformative technology.

Now Russian engineers Leonid and Sergey Plekhanov say it's time to pick up where Tesla left off. After all, it is 100 years later in a Wi-Fi-obsessed era. The brothers, both graduates of Moscow Institute of Physics and Technology, or the "Russian MIT", crowdfunded USD 46,000 to help research their Planetary Energy Transmitter. The basic idea is to pump electricity into buildings via 10-story-tall transmitting towers, which can handle power surges in excess of 3 million volts. The towers send power to wireless receivers by creating currents in the ground. (US electrical wall sockets, by comparison, are rated at 110 volts.)

Makeshift caught up with Leonid about the possibility of clean, wire-free energy amidst public fear of creating a planetary microwave oven.

Makeshift: What inspired you to carry forward Tesla's work?
LP: Tesla's skills in practical experimentation were amazing. Through our own research, we concluded that his basic premise can actually work. Since we see this as extremely important and see the potential to really change the technological landscape of the future, we decided to start building the tower. It will be worth the money, time, and energy to bring this to reality.

Besides the huge cost and technical hurdles, what are your biggest challenges?
The main issue is the halo of mystery and secrecy that has been surrounding Tesla for a long while. Energy transmission remains a

very complex issue, and we are dealing with very new construction and technological challenges, based on high-voltage physics and planetary resonance (a phenomenon related to gravity). We have to break through the wall of mistrust. This will take a lot of time and require a great deal of effort, patience, and energy. However, I think that once we get irrefutable proof that the energy transmitter can work, the situation will radically change.

What are the key differences between Tesla's designs and the Planetary Energy Transmitter?
Using new materials, computers, and electronics, we can design a lighter-weight construction. Tesla's Wardenclyffe tower weighed more than 60 tonnes, while our construction will be only around 2 tonnes. All other parameters—frequency, voltage, power—are very close to the ones that Tesla used.

How will the device generate, transmit, and receive electricity?
In simple words, the energy transmission happens in the same way as with usual transmis-

sion lines. Except the wire in this case is the superficial layer of the Earth, at depths of about 100 to 1,000 meters, together with the Earth-Ionosphere waveguide (the phenomenon in which radio waves are transmitted between the ground and upper atmosphere). The Tower-Transmitter literally "oscillates" the currents that flow across the ground toward different points, and the Tower-Receiver "collects" the energy from these currents.

How will it improve the way we live and work?
Firstly, there will be such a great opportunity to transfer energy to areas with difficult access. Secondly, we can make energy much cheaper, because transmission losses via regular wires are huge, as are the costs of infrastructure and maintenance. Lastly, it will make it easier to use cleaner sources of energy, such as wind and solar power. Some of the best wind and solar resources are located far away from the consumption centers, and this is a real barrier for green energy. (Think of a blazing but isolated California desert or a wind-swept prairie in the middle of nowhere.) If we can solve this challenge of safe and controlled energy transmission, then we can bring renewable energy projects to life. As a long-term vision, we really believe it's possible to use the desert's energy for the sake of all mankind. The availability of energy sources is one of the most important factors in global politics.

Nikola Tesla has many other fans. Do you consider yourselves part of the Tesla community?
We are not exactly Tesla's fans. We are scientists, and we don't spend time at forums or events of any kind. First of all, we don't have time for that. Secondly, there are very few experienced researchers in such communities, so it is very difficult to find someone who can understand details of our work and collaborate. We concentrate on what we do. ⊗

—GE x Makeshift

Overcoming Africa's Power Challenges

BY LORRAINE BOLSINGER

Africa is home to 12 of the 20 fastest-growing economies; its strong manufacturing, services, and technology sectors are fueling economies around the globe. And many of these economies are achieving success without being able to make full use of all its resources because access to electricity is still lacking in many areas.

Approximately 600 million people in Africa do not have access to power. This situation takes a toll on human health, access to opportunity, and economic growth.

Developing reliable power supplies across the continent is therefore a global priority and a critical necessity to ensure African nations can reach their economic and human potential. To realize reliable power across Africa, a host of partners—governments, non-governmental

organizations, the private sector, the global investment community—must work together to transform Africa's power challenges into power opportunities. The good news is that the hurdles before us are not insurmountable, and with the proper steps and sustained commitment, these goals can be achieved.

Today, three primary challenges exist that, if addressed in smart ways, means energy can flow across Africa more easily to more areas: fuel availability, speed to power, and affordability and financing.

Despite the fact that Africa is blessed with rich energy resources, fuel availability is a problem in many parts of the continent. Africa's abundant natural gas resources aren't always co-located with power generation sites. This means that while the raw ingredients needed to support sustained growth are in place, in many cases the technology is not yet there to convert those resources into electricity. In Kenya, for example, independent power producers and smaller power generation companies are using available resources—such as agricultural waste—to generate local power

using engines that are capable of running on a wide range of fuels.

With a high, urgent demand for electricity across Africa, speed to power is another challenge that must be addressed. It can take years to develop the necessary infrastructure to deliver power across large—at times, remote—areas. Technologies like distributed power—flexible, decentralized power systems—can be installed in a matter of weeks, reducing wait time and speeding up economic activity. Local generation projects are scalable, too—if one engine is installed and the electricity need rises in a community later on, additional engines can be added relatively quickly.

While we are seeing that the technology exists to solve specific problems, economic challenges remain in terms of affordability and financing for power projects. Here, too, there is a bright note. For smaller-scale projects with gas engines and gas turbines, lower installed costs and smaller increments open up more financing choices and bring power to African countries quicker. These smaller distributed power and local generation projects do not require transmission infrastructure, also known as a power grid, that is both costly and complex.

Partnerships in combination with technologies like distributed power can bring electricity to African countries at speeds once unheard of.

Lorraine Bolsinger is President & CEO of GE Power & Water's Distributed Power business.

Learn more about GE's Distributed Power business at ge-distributedpower.com

Africa50 Infrastructure Fund
About USD 385 billion is needed by 2030 to fill the power gap. Africa50 is a new fund aimed at mobilizing local and external resources.

bit.ly/ZfQeOk

Banda Gas-to-Power Project
The Banda Project harnesses offshore gas fields to produce power to provide affordable energy for 7 million people in Mauritania, Mali, and Senegal.

bit.ly/8mTAkDF

Harnessing the Wind
GE's Kinangop and Kipeto Wind Farms are part of an effort to add 500 MW of wind power to Kenya's energy mix.

bit.ly/3Av62YJ

Closing Africa's Energy Poverty Gap

BY TODD MOSS & BETH SCHWANKE

Two out of three people in Sub-Saharan Africa—that's nearly 600 million people—live today without access to electricity. As incomes and economies grow in Africa, and they are both growing quickly, this will generate massive demand for power access.

Optimism around the region's booming economies is proliferating, with good reason. But without dramatically increased access to electricity across the continent, these rosy forecasts can't last. To put the scale of the access problem in perspective, Todd's energy-efficient, single-family refrigerator uses nine times more electricity in a year than the average person in Ethiopia.

Consumption inequality aside, the impact of this continent-wide energy poverty on individual lives and economies is pervasive and crippling. Without reliable access to electricity, doctors can't refrigerate vaccines. Students can't study at night. Farmers can't prevent the spoilage of their harvests. And businesses can't grow.

Congress has the opportunity to begin to change this, by passing the Energize Africa Act, co-sponsored by Senators Robert Menendez (D-NJ) and Bob Corker (R-TN). The House has already passed the companion legislation, Electrify Africa. The Energize Africa Act would cement President Obama's Power Africa initiative to increase electricity access in six African countries through leveraging partnerships with the private sector. At the US-Africa Leaders Summit in August, the president announced a tripling of the initial targets—aiming to create access for at least 60 million new households and businesses, which could mean that up to 300 million people would acquire reliable access to electricity.

This would be a remarkable and game-changing result for the individuals and businesses gaining access to reliable electricity, for U.S.-Africa relations, and for U.S. businesses hoping to invest in Africa.

But as much as we're thrilled by the president's Power Africa initiative and hope Congress will pass Energize Africa—ideally with the bold targets of President Obama's expansion—the U.S. government must now work to make this vision a reality.

Implementation won't be easy. Recognizing that the total annual energy consumption of many African citizens barely hits that of most Americans' refrigerators, the United States should end its restrictions on investing in natural gas for low-emitting, energy-poor countries. Allowing the Overseas Private Investment Corporation (OPIC) to invest in natural gas in these countries would provide electricity to millions more people and help respond to the biggest constraint to growth for Africa's private sector. The American economy is benefiting greatly from natural gas, and African nations should be allowed to do the same, using their own local gas reserves to generate electricity at home.

Both the development need and the business opportunity are there — let's hope the administration and Congress will help the U.S. private sector be in a position to help close Africa's energy poverty gap.

Todd Moss is the Chief Operating Officer and Senior Fellow at the Center for Global Development; Beth Schwanke is Senior Policy Counsel at CGD.

Fostering a More Sustainable Africa

BY LORENZO SIMONELLI

Africa has quickly become one of the world's fastest-growing regions. Yet growth without consistency will not allow African countries to reach full potential and be competitive in a global economy. As a result, Africa's partners can play a role by helping to create an infrastructure for lasting and inclusive growth — especially to address the continent's energy gap.

That's when what GE terms "localization" comes in. Localization focuses more on capacity building — in human capital growth, supply chain development and partnership with local organizations and businesses for talent and infrastructure development.

To GE, localization is a strategy, not just a requirement. Localization enables growth in the communities in which we work, while increasing our productivity. As a global company, GE has the unique opportunity to have a well-rounded economic impact on the regions where we operate. For Africans, that means hiring local staff and providing development opportunities.

Our efforts can be summed up in three words: grow, build,

localize. GE grows through local development and infrastructure support, builds productive partnerships and deepens its local presence. GE has already made much progress across Africa—we are a multinational company but strive to be local in all of our markets. One of our major priorities is to foster the development of human capital, and we do that through partnerships with local education partners and governments.

For example, GE has partnered with the African Leadership Academy to give out scholarships and provide professional development opportunities to African students. Most recently, GE Oil & Gas has committed to giving USD 60,000 in school supplies and skills training to local students in Angola.

Supporting and growing local supply chains with special focus on developing local partners—especially small- and medium-sized enterprises—also will have a multiplying effect on investments across Africa. As GE partners with local companies, supporting tech transfer through manufacturing process improvements, training

and management engagement all help to support and grow local innovation and entrepreneurship.

For example, just last year, GE unveiled plans to build a multi-modal facility in Calabar, Nigeria. This plant will generate 2,300 new jobs in Nigeria—300 directly and around 2,000 across the supply chain. Management and staff of that facility will be 90 percent Nigerian. Investments like this lay the foundation for knowledge and technology transfer to Nigerian sub-suppliers, academic institutions and people, which leads to greater development of in-country capabilities.

Localization is one of the biggest growth enablers. With this attitude, we are helping Africa build a future of increased— and sustainable—growth.

Lorenzo Simonelli is President and CEO of GE Oil & Gas.

FIGHTING ENERGY POVERTY
Sub-Saharan Africa is resource-rich—especially with recent oil and gas discoveries—but poor energy infrastructure is stunting development.

600 million
number of people who lack access to electricity

56 days
average days/year manufacturers lose power

2.1 percent
average cost to GDP from power shutdowns

"It starts out f
tickles. Then y
cramp up. And
can't move."

eeling like
our arms
then you

USING IT | ISSUE 10 | POWERING UP

WORDS
ROSE ODENGO

PHOTO
AMUNGA ESHUCHI

KENYA | ANNUAL COST OF POOR SANITATION
USD 324 MILLION | OPEN DEFECATION
13% OF POPULATION

Human filth fuels warm water and cooking stoves inside Nairobi's biggest slum
—Poo Power

An elderly man in a blue shirt and grey pants kicks off his faded pink flip-flops. Abubakar Andama Oluoc passes him by, lugging a blue plastic basin on her way to a two-burner gas stove. Atop it sits a colossal pot brimming with hot water. She scoops the water into the basin, and the man nods his head. He takes it and heaves it toward a door labeled "Shower".

21-year-old Abubakar heads the Kibera Kids Youth Organization (KIDYOT), which operates this "biocenter" in Kibera, the largest informal settlement in Nairobi and one of the biggest in Africa. In the large, cylindrical facility are toilets, showers, and gas stoves. The whole thing runs on poop fumes.

When residents come to use the toilets, their 'human investments' fall into a 31,000-liter bio-digester underground. Inside the oxygen-free receptacle, a process called anaerobic digestion takes place, and the waste breaks down into mostly methane gas. The methane is piped throughout the facility to fire up stoves, which heat water for showers and communal cooking.

Maureen Achieng' Opondo cooks up fried food for her street stand here. The 23-year-old pays 5 shillings (USD 0.06) per day to use a stove in the adjacent kitchen room. Pipes transport gas from the bio-digester directly into the burners, with valves to control the output. She saves about 100 shillings (USD 1.13) per day now since she no longer has to buy charcoal. "Business is better," she says.

Kibera's biocenter is one of nearly 70 facilities run by different groups in informal settlements across Kenya. KIDYOT has about 90 members, mostly between 10 and 30 years old. Its goal is to not only improve the area's sanitation but also generate an income for the slum's residents—something other than "low-paying manual labor and construction work", says member Collins Liko.

Along with cooking costs, the group charges 5 shillings (USD 0.06) to take a seat in the bathroom. A shower costs 10 shillings, plus an extra

5 shillings if you want hot water. On the second floor, you can pay to watch football broadcast on TV in the community space. Each month, the biocenter rakes in about 60,000 shillings (USD 705), and the profits are reinvested into the community.

KIDYOT was formed eight years ago by community organizers in Kibera, who raised money from Umande Trust, a nonprofit group, to buy land for a biocenter. KIDYOT received some outside technical support to build the facility, though Kibera residents handled most of the construction. Abubakar, Collins, and others dug the foundation for the building, transforming themselves into masons virtually overnight. Steve Biko, a 22-year-old self-taught electrician, wired the place by himself.

But when the facility opened in 2010, residents were largely uninterested. "Open defecation was very high," Collins explains. Many people used plastic nylon bags, known as "flying toilets", and would toss them in ditches or along the roadside once they were filled. It was a challenge to shift people from "doing it for free".

And the idea of using human waste to fire up food kept some people from the stoves. "People used to say cooking within a toilet...that food is inedible," says Abubakar, who, along with running the biocenter, recently became a junior police officer.

KIDYOT held meetings across the slum to explain how the new toilets could help prevent disease and churn out some income. Within four months, the facility began making methane biogas, and now the center averages 300 to 500 visitors each day.

"The people who use it consume alcohol, and that is an advantage," jokes Japheth Igaiza, a 27-year-old group member. He says the high-alcohol waste boosts production of methane captured by the digester.

Even after adoption ramped up, KIDYOT continued to face challenges. Crime and

Outside the Kibera Kids Youth Organization, home of the biocenter.

insecurity is high in Kibera, and people have been raped or mugged on their way to the bathroom. So now it operates daily from 6 a.m. to 7 p.m. Their initial plans to share revenue with the community also flopped. Instead, the group began investing in skills, lending money to young people to earn university degrees in specific fields. Steve, the electrician, and Collins both used their family's proceeds to pay for high school. Steve is now studying business and teaching in Kibera, while Collins holds a degree in community development.

After investing in skills, remaining profits are set aside for new projects. Over the next decade, KIDYOT wants to build more biocenters and run a biogas and fertilizer processing plant. With it, Kibera can sell fertilizer and energy cheaper than conventional charcoal and paraffin supplies, Japheth says. The group will need a biogas reactor worth 2.5 million shillings (USD 30,000) to help the facility break down waste and produce the gas. From there, all they'll need is a bit more fecal matter. ⊗

	WORDS & PHOTO	ILLUSTRATION
	ALEX POTTER	ALICE PATTULLO
YEMEN	EMPLOYMENT IN AGRICULTURE	NAT'L UNEMPLOYMENT
	54% OF EMPLOYMENT	40%

Qat fuels a multimillion-dollar industry in Yemen and the daily lives of nearly all its citizens
—Leafy Buzz

Abdullah al Areeqi spends most afternoons in the back seat of his Toyota pickup truck, hawking plastic baggies of green leaves in Yemen's capital of Sana'a. Pouches dangle from the truck's ceiling and cluster in his lap; still more are stacked in the bed behind him. He haggles over the price with all of his customers, who take the leaves and shove them deep into their cheeks. Throughout the day, they'll nurse their golf ball-size bulges while working, lounging, fighting—just about anything except eating and praying.

Abdullah is one of the millions of informal *qat* (also "khat") workers in Yemen, a country where roughly 90 percent of all men and over half of women use qat. Many can be seen in a typical qat-chewing pose: the lean. Deliverymen recline in the trunks of their cars, carpenters back into unfinished dressers, seed salesmen nestle into their bags of grain, all aiming to con-trol the spit the chewing produces. As they lean, qat's amphetamine-like effects kick in. Workers say it gives them power to push through long hours, and many people use it to smooth the awkward edges of social gatherings.

"Qat helps you focus," Abdullah explains from inside his truck-turned-shop in Tahrir, the main commercial square of Sana'a. "When you need to do one task at a time and work hard on it, qat is great for that."

Qat is far more than a physical stimulant. The leaf is propelling the black market economy in Yemen, the poorest country in the Arab world. Vendors typically sell billions of riyals worth of leaves—or millions of US dollars—across the country each day; this number doesn't include money made by other links in the supply chain, like village workers who pick the leaves and tribesmen who truck them from farm to market.

A slice of life in Yemen's highlands, where some 90% of men and 50% of women are thought to chew qat.

A growing number of Yemenis and international groups, however, are starting to see this as a scourge—not an economic boon. Qat leaves are lucrative, so they're pushing out more exportable crops like fruits and coffee. They're also sucking up 40 percent of the nation's dwindling water supplies. The World Health Organization

says that despite its caffeine-like buzz qat is actually causing Yemen's workforce to power down as laborers, lose sleep, or devote vital working hours to chewing qat.

Because of public health and environmental concerns, a handful of countries have made it illegal to grow and chew qat, including most

QAT COMPARED

In Yemen alone, there are dozens of types of qat, most named for the region in which they grow. Each has a unique look and effect, depending on its region's climate and elevation. Here are three of the most-chewed leaves with their winter and summer price tags for an afternoon chew:

(A) Ansi

Grown in the relatively warm midlands, at elevations around 1,500 meters, Ansi's large leaves are resistant to heat, making it popular in humid areas like Hudaydah, Aden, and Socotra.

❄ 3,500 riyals (USD 17)

☀ 1,000 riyals (USD 5)

(B) Arhabi

Arhabi has the tiniest leaves, 1-3 centimeters long, and chewers pick the most delicate a few at a time, making the bag last for hours. Grown in the high and dry mountain areas of Arhab, northeast of Sana'a, city-dwellers like this qat for its strong high but easy let-down.

❄ 5,000 riyals (USD 25)

☀ 2,500 riyals (USD 12)

(C) Sawti

The strongest and cheapest of all, Sawti is the qat of the masses, popular among laborers with tough hours. It brings the chewer up quickly and drops down even faster. The short and knobby stalks have small and delicate leaves, one reason they are wrapped in banana leaves.

❄ 1,000 riyals (USD 5)

☀ 500 riyals (USD 2.5)

recently Canada and the United Kingdom. Yemen's neighbor, Saudi Arabia, also bans qat, making it harder for Yemenis to push their product next door. Saudi border guards seize millions of kilograms of Yemeni qat each year, some of which comes stuffed in smugglers' shirts and pants.

None of this seems to have made a dent in Haraz's qat business. The misty highland region west of Sana'a is blanketed with stubby *Catha edulis* shrubs along terraced mountainsides. As visitors drive up to each village, groups of young boys run onto the road, lugging their fathers' harvest in bags or in bundles as big as their bodies. "This is the best qat. I just pulled it an hour ago," they call out over each other. "I'm selling for only 2,000 riyals (USD 9)—less than what you'll get down the road." Nearly every driver declines and gently taps the gas, until a pair of toothpick legs comes running after him, ready to haggle.

And despite unease about qat, the leaves haven't lost their social allure. Fine qat, akin to expensive wines and cigars in the West, remains a status symbol; at weddings, influential families pass out top-quality and high-energy qat to

> Fine qat, akin to expensive wines and cigars in the West, remains a status symbol.

guests. Power brokers like politicians, sheikhs, and religious leaders chew qat to promote decision-making and negotiate business—a process known as *Sa'ah solimaniyah*, or the hour of discussion. Another stage of qat-chewing is *sa'ah al hudu'*, or the hour of relaxing.

Quality of qat is essential; wilted qat is as useful as moldy bread to even a novice chewer. Since qat spoils quickly in Yemen's hot climate, vendors experiment with the packaging to extend the shelf life of the leaves.

At the Tahrir market in Sana'a, Abdul Rahman wraps his haul in folded stalks of bamboo, creating tight-rolled packages. "This kind of qat is special. It's very strong, so we try to keep it fresh," he explains, sitting on the ground near a street-side restaurant. The kind of qat he's talking about is called *Sawti*, a cheaper variety notorious for causing strong highs and sleep deprivation. There's also *Hamdani,* which gives a quick boost but dies out quickly, and *Ansi,* which has a slow, burning energy that lasts for hours.

Even trickier than keeping leaves crisp is chewing abroad. Smuggling-friendly versions are dried out (made into *ya'bis*) and packed tightly, making qat easier to hide from airport security in places like the UK and US (where the legality of the plant hovers in a grey area). This doesn't inhibit popularity though. On a recent trip to New York City, I encountered a number of Yemenis chewing the dried brown leaves in a café. "It is not as tasty," one man remarked, "but it still has the same effect." ⊗

WORDS & PHOTOS
JAMES FREDRICK

ILLUSTRATIONS
RONA BINAY

MINIMUM DETECTABLE SHOCK
1 MA AC OR 5 MA DC

HEART ATTACK TRIGGER POINT
30 MA AC OR 300-500 MA DC

Mexico City residents pay
toqueros for electrical shocks strong
enough to knock out a dog
—Streetside Shocks

Carlos Victorino clutches a stiff brown
briefcase and clinks together two metal rods as
he wanders the dusky streets of Mexico City's
historic *centro*. He eyeballs the families and
revelers out on a busy Saturday night, beckon-
ing them to approach with the clink-clink-clink
of his hand. For a small fee, he'll fill them with
enough electricity to knock out a small dog.

"It feels like adrenaline," says Marco Antonio Camacho, who just received a jolt from
the rods that link back to the battery in Carlos's
briefcase. Marco Antonio and his family sit
together, still shaking out their arms after paying for Carlos's services, while mariachi music
rings out nearby.

In Mexico, paying for a shock—called a *toque*,
or hit—is an enduring pastime. Carlos is about
to turn 60, and he's been at it since he was 14. It
doesn't pay much, but it's enough to get by. So
far, he's earned about 130 pesos (USD 10) from
the Camacho family, plus a quick USD 8 from
another group earlier that night.

Carlos's setup seems fairly inconspicuous at
first glance. Most of what's visible in his flipped-
open briefcase are cigars: Cohibas of dubious
provenance and some cheap ones that mainly
serve as decoration. Tucked in the bottom-left-
hand corner is a power switch and a one-to-ten
dial emblazoned with a flashing skull and cross-
bones, alongside inputs for two electric cables,
which connect to two cylindrical metal handles
he holds between his fingers.

Inside a little box are six rechargeable
AA batteries, an inverter, and a transformer
that controls the voltage, which can reach up

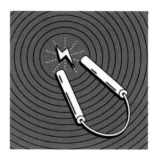

SHOCK FACTOR
Running electrical currents
through the human body
has its practical, though
sometimes questionable,
uses. Here's how they
stack up:

Electroconvulsive
Therapy
Induces seizure for relief
from mental illness

⚡ 0.8 amps over
several seconds

Electrosurgical Unit
Induces a small current
to help cut skin

⚡ 10 amps at high
frequency

Taser
Stuns aggressors for
personal defense

⚡ 0.003 amps at
high voltage

Electric Chair
Injects lethal doses
of electricity

⚡ 6 amps for
30–60 seconds

Cigars on display and toques
in hand, Carlos looks for
clients to shock near Plaza
Garibaldi in Mexico City.

to 100 volts. The toque is the more controlled version of sticking your finger in an electrical outlet.

Carlos learned how to build a toque box as a teenager and has outfitted several briefcases throughout his career. The technology hasn't evolved much, and most of the remaining *toqueros* still use an old-school setup like Carlos, making the crafty mechanics work with rusty parts.

"It's tough—you can't get these parts anymore," he says. "If you were to find them, you would have to invest 8,000 pesos (USD 600) to make one."

Adventurous passersby can do toques alone or in a group. If you're going solo, grasp one handle in each hand—the positive and negative charges. See how high Carlos can ratchet up the voltage before you scream out "*Ya, ya, yaaaaa! Enough!*" This costs USD 1. Your friend can pay another dollar to try to beat your voltage. If you're out with friends or unwitting children, form a semicircle and grab hands; two people at the end will each grab a handle. Carlos dials

"It starts out feeling like tickles...
And then everything tightens up.
You can't move. You can't let go."

up the voltage until someone breaks the human-conducted current. This costs about USD 2 for every turn.

Before the toque begins, the metal handles are cold and dull. Then Carlos flips the switch, and you hear a buzz. You get nervous and start speaking higher. You giggle. The dial is still at zero.

"It starts out feeling like tickles," says Sergio, a tipsy 20-something who reached five out of 10 on the dial. "Then your arms almost begin to cramp up. And then everything tightens up. You can't move. You can't let go. You're stuck." He's still buzzed and giggling after the shock.

Sergio says the toque is a classic Mexico City experience. "It's a tradition thing: come see mariachis, drink, do the toques. It's fun." Plaza Garibaldi, where Carlos hustles his shock sticks,

TURN IT UP
Here's what happens at each stage when a toquero cranks up the zap:

1. Your palms tickle

2. Your hands reflexively grip the handles

3. Your wrists curl inward and you laugh

4. Your biceps contract and arms hug your chest

5. Your arms are mostly immobile and laughing turns to grimacing

6. You yell and grunt uncontrollably

7. Your arms are completely immobile and your mind is stunned

8. You scream and your body holds on for dear life

Carlos's conductor sticks, up close and ready to shock.

is the land of the mariachi, and dozens of musical groups still gather at the plaza every night. Part festive and part melancholy, they're paid per song by starry lovers, bellowing drunks, and nostalgic families.

Carlos sees himself as part of Mexico's old-school toquero tradition, though the trade predates him. He says it probably began in the Mexican cantina culture of bravado.

"If there were four or five of us sitting here, we'd start placing bets to see who pays for the drinks," he explains. "So we do a few toques and whoever gets the least pays the tab."

Plaza Garibaldi used to feel like the boisterous cantina itself. It's been the city's mariachi plaza for almost a century and, for most of that time, it was a plaza of debauchery and petty crime, given its proximity to Mexico City's roughest barrio, Tepito.

A couple years ago, however, the city government "rescued" Garibaldi, banning open containers of alcohol and clamping down on crime. While families and tourists welcomed the changes, Carlos had thrived in the unfettered mess of old Garibaldi.

"It was a very abrupt and ugly change, mostly for those of us who work here," he says. "20 years ago there were 25 of us." Today, just four toqueros remain, and Carlos is the oldest.

His wife, Juana, became a toquero a couple years ago when Carlos's work took a dive. On a good night, they can make USD 50 together. Since Garibaldi was cleaned up, he only works Thursday through Sunday. They still make enough to support their four children.

Despite working until 5 a.m., putting up with drunken insults, and pacing around a still-raucous plaza, Carlos can't see himself moving on from Garibaldi or the toques.

"If I were to get another job, I'd be told to do this or do that, and I'd have to do it," he says. "With the years I have, I don't think I could get used to a boss."

He wanders off under the fluorescent streetlamps, the tinny clinking of the handles fading with him. ⊗

▶ MAKESHIFT ON AIR
Check mkshft.org for our upcoming video featuring Mexico City's toqueros.

Photographer Tara Rice recalls a moment when the sun kept her energy alive
—Solar Boom

The only sound I heard as I trekked into the village was the scratchy thumping of a boom-box. The rhythmic beat of a West African band lulled me into a contentedness; I had almost forgotten how strange it was to hear record-ed music playing in such a remote part of the world. Some 30 miles south of Timbuktu, where the Sahara melts into lush rice paddies and the Niger River crawls around oasis-like islands, scarce (and expensive) generators come closest to anything resembling an electrical grid. The remote villages live off of the river and the imports being hauled into Mali in large, colorful boats. Kids run past with massive plumes of hay balanced on their heads; donkeys wait patiently in the shade for the 46-degree sun to set.

As I turned a corner, the sound grew louder, then crackled, then gave out completely. With a great sense of urgency a boy ran in front of me in the direction from where the music was coming. It seemed like the whole village paused in that moment. Fiddling with an intricate weave of orange and grey cord that connected a solar panel of unknown origin to the cable of the boom box, he managed to resurrect the mu-sic—an act followed by an enthusiastic applause from his friends. The rhythmic beating of the drums resumed to the speaker, as did the boy and his friends to their work, busily forming bricks to bake under the intense sun. I walked on, soaking in the beautiful melodies and a newfound appreciation for human ingenuity in such an isolated environment. ⊗

Found sounds and a
sun-blasted stereo.

CHINA COAL BASE TOUR

This virtual tour takes you through the world's largest fossil fuel development project. Flipping through sites on Google Earth's 3D globe, you can visit the approximate locations of 14 planned secretive complexes across China's countryside designed to convert coal into synthetic gas, liquid fuel, and other products.

Free

bit.ly/3qAWham

DREAM BIG LIVE TINY

If you're longing for a simpler lifestyle, this workshop is for you. Tiny house builder Tumbleweed Houses will walk you through designing and planning your own mini mansion, which takes less energy to build and control temperature. You'll be bucking the American trend—the average American lives in more than twice the space of Brits.

USD 329

Various cities, United States

tumbleweedhouses.com

TAMMY STROBEL

HOMEMADE ENERGY DRINK

Craving a more personalized jolt to fend off that 2 p.m. feeling? Guzzle down Caffeine Informer's DIY energy drink recipe. Mix its suggested caffeine sources, flavorings, and herbs for your perfect buzz. And for those who want to spin up a business, the recipe advises on manufacturing rates and questionable marketing techniques.

USD 1.23/can

bit.ly/WHPrqM

HVERAGERðI GEOTHERMAL PARK

The self-proclaimed hot spring capital of the world—in a country that runs on geothermal energy—Hveragerði is a wonderful site for "earth cooking", a culinary experience that takes place on your nearest floor or riverbed. After boiling an egg in the stream, tour the geothermal plant and take a natural clay foot bath in the mud.

Free to visit

Hveragerði, Iceland

hveragerdi.is

RYAN TAYLOR

THE NEW 49'ERS

For the amateur miner seeking adventure, gold prospecting club The New 49'ers provides community and the thrill of profitable discovery. Their 100-kilometer prospecting trip through North Carolina guarantees you'll strike gold—and keep it. Non-members can join for one day for free.

USD 100/year

Various sites, United States

goldgold.com

JANOTHIRD

SMARTTHINGS

What did your light bulb say to the air conditioner? Find out with SmartThings, the open platform that connects your home's devices via the Internet, so you can control and monitor them. Originally Kickstarted at USD 1.2 million, the platform consists of a hub, sensors that detect events like motion and open doors, and devices you can control, like smart outlets to conserve energy.

USD 199 for starter kit

smartthings.com

SMART METER HACKING

Perhaps you already have a smart device, installed by your water or power company, and you want to tamper with it to save cash or perform espionage. A 2012 workshop at DefCon, the annual summit for hackers and undercover CIA agents, called "Looking in to the Eye of the Meter" explained the process. And now the talk is available online for the whole world's eyes.

Free

bit.ly/5opcdZJ